ASHES

RAHMA JIMOH

This is a work of fiction. All names, characters, places, and incidents are a product of the author's imagination. Any resemblance to real events or persons, living or dead, is entirely coincidental.

Published by Akashic Books

ISBN: 978-1-63614-245-6

Printed in China
First printing

EU Authorized Representative details:
Easy Access System Europe
Mustamäe tee 50, 10621 Tallinn, Estonia
gpsr.request@easproject.com

Akashic Books
Instagram, X, Facebook: AkashicBooks
info@akashicbooks.com
www.akashicbooks.com

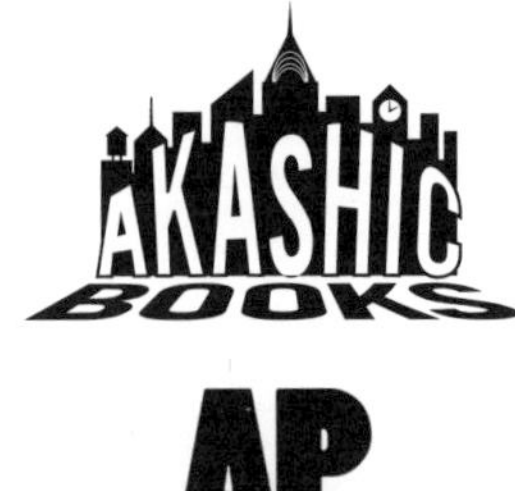

African Poetry Book Fund
Brown University
10 Prospect Street
Box A
Providence, RI 02912

For the girl weeping while writing her first poems after the system first failed her. For all the times she screamed for help in muffled language and indirect messages. For the light and friend that poetry will continue to be. For all the people who tried to be poetry.

TABLE OF CONTENTS

PREFACE

by Safia Jama

The poems in Rahma Jimoh's *Ashes* create a leveling landscape where memories of a Nigerian homeland run thick. Nigeria, often personified as a woman, is contending not only with pollution, but "desecration" ("The City's Back Door"). Such diction is not without grounds. In the title poem, "Ashes," Jimoh's speaker conjures backroom bargains in a land rich in oil:

> I imagine the President's shady
> promises about compensation.
> Trucks ply broken roads.
> Afar, gloomy smoke levitates
> toward heaven.

Despite the bleakness, Jimoh's verses make space for humor and wit:

> Nothing works here until there's
> some damage. It is a bargain of
> survival without a written treaty
> that Nigeria won't still burn you.
>
> ("Ashes")

The speaker sums up the logic of certain programs that depend upon ongoing, and supposedly inevitable, ecological damage.

The rage in these poems is real and justified. Yet more often, a palpable heartache forms the backbeat to Jimoh's cri de coeur. The choice of leaving one's homeland is likened to leaving a destructive romance:

This country kills me daily
and my body is now dead from dying.
I try, I want to fall in love with her.

Again, my memory ricochets to
the boy from college, he too broke me.

("The City's Back Door")

Yearning for a love that is hard to find, the speaker reaches instead for the goal of seeing and affirming oneself. The collection's opening poem is dedicated "*For you.*" Hovering above the dedication, the poem's title, "Playacting," jars with such tenderness: there's pain there. Nonetheless, Jimoh's speaker risks vulnerability with each successive line.

Jimoh, a poet and storyteller from Nigeria, claims and protects spaces in her world that are encroached upon. The end-stopped lines include caesuras, allowing for more room:

you hold up and pour into others.
you stretch. in hopes that the emptiness you feel fills.
you collect spaces. you light up the night.
and show up even as the world breaks your strength.

("Playacting")

Despite the "light" contained in this poem, which opens the collection, there is no premature redemption to be found in those that follow. Instead, Jimoh employs language in playful and ingenious ways, allowing the reader to experience spaciousness. Using a multiplicity of voices and forms, the collection does not adhere to any one style and therefore reveals a poetry born of necessity.

Jimoh shines her light upon Nigeria's police brutality and violent suppression of young people; any perceived deviation from the norm can lead to sudden arrest or worse. The speaker in "The Lekki Toll Gate," referencing the events of October 2020, bears witness to such violence while grasping for a spiritual meaning that remains elusive: "Prayer in my country is a loud battle / with invisible enemies."

The poet seems to find spirituality in nature in the poem "Phantom." Notice how Jimoh's speaker builds an argument for peace from the vantage point of a ghostly voice:

> I pour into others and the sea
> mirrors the sky's vastness.
> Beyond the shores, I see people
> being people; not a single
> White, Black, Yoruba, Muslim, or Atheist.

The speaker's voice rises above religious conflict, locating a spiritual geography where fear of the other gives way to the serenity of the sea: "I transcend to water."

Jimoh's poems work to dissolve—or at least name—seemingly insoluble problems. They retaliate against despair with casual levity, as in the poem "It's Smoky." They also expose those who take sadistic pleasure in harming children: in "Land Mine," Jimoh's speaker asks, "What is the future shape of our country / —our land mine that takes joy / in playing with the ashes of its youths?" Conversely, in her poem "Hide and Seek," Jimoh invites us to consider the experiences of children who must hide to remain safe. Her speaker gets to the heart of this topic by asking, "Do you know how high you have to / count to be hidden for five years?"

The realities of gender-based violence and inequality infuse the atmosphere of *Ashes*. "Consequence" concludes with the poem claustrophobically folding in on itself:

Every man will become guilty
of something before a certain age,
before their appointed time. I wonder
what guilt will eat me into aging.

Notice how Jimoh's speaker nestles in the center of the poem, a restless sleeper under pressure to remain intact:

I turn over on my bed at night
after keeping everyone's expectation
of me under my pillow—
to sleep on.

Rahma Jimoh's visions of smoke and ash show us that before reform can happen, there must be a faithful rendering of the truth, as well as a necessary razing of untruths. Jimoh's verses burn with a purifying smoke. Out of the ashes, what can be reimagined? Remade?

PLAYACTING

For you.

water holds you in its long hands.
and the lines on your palms open pathways for you.
you squeeze into shallow spaces.
no room to breathe, swim or drown.
in silence, you burn.
your mouth, dry, eats hours and hours of sleep.
how long will you water these pains?
your soul, like your voice, tender, flower tendrils.
musical. tissue.   you conceal scars in your back pockets.
I catch the tenor of your breath.
the color of your emotions.
the shape of your pain.
you mask happiness while your insides scream.
you revise tales to escape your tongue.
while your heart screams, threatening to break free.
this I know—in my refusal to buy into your playacting.
you hold up and pour into others.
you stretch. in hopes that the emptiness you feel fills.
you collect spaces. you light up the night.
and show up even as the world breaks your strength.
you, I know, are water. how you pour yourself into others.
flow into arms serving light.
travel into spaces, circling, circling every chasm.
this I know to make you pure.

CONSEQUENCE

Every man will become guilty
of something before a certain age,
before their appointed time. I wonder
what guilt will eat me into aging.

I think of the decisions
or indecisions
my father made to arrive here
here, at this junction.

I turn over on my bed at night
after keeping everyone's expectation
of me under my pillow—
to sleep on.

I'm only trying to wake up
the next morning, my mind
still in its right place.
I'm only trying to wake up

the next morning, a sane person
unworried about the dollar rising like flour
in the oven. I'm only trying to wake up
to an emptied mind and stocked kitchen.

Every man will become guilty
of something before a certain age,
before their appointed time. I wonder
what guilt will eat me into aging.

NINETY-NINE (99)

My 99-year-old grandfather covers his face.
He does not want us to stare at his wrinkles.
My 99-year-old grandfather waits hopefully.

Listens to the radio while he waits until
the morning when the radio churns out:
99 workers have died in a BRT bus collision.

My grandfather counts 99 with
his fingers. Asks me how old Nigeria will be
in October. I tell him, "63, you're over

30 years older and wiser." My grandfather
sighs, sleeps, and doesn't wake again.
My grandfather travels with 99 others.

HIDE AND SEEK

Do you know how high you have to
count to be hidden for five years?
Hell, no one told five-year-olds to hush
and listen closely as death runs by.
My mother's palms are up together,
shaking in dismay like dried leaves
on a turbulent sea. Her lips quivering
as her eyes gear toward the sky
begging Ar-Rahman to keep us safe
from all that quakes this place.
Not everyone who witnesses the start
of a war lives long enough to watch
its flames die out. I watched,
as they dragged an old man by his hair
whose only crime was being ~~different~~.
I shiver, wondering if I will witness this
happening to my father too.
In Palestine, Sudan, Maiduguri, and Jos,
many innocent lives get cut short
for the difference in tongue, belief,
or color. I think of similarities
as bulletproof. Our bruised hearts,
look at the world, see, it aches.
Just yesterday, my mother hummed
as she made potatoes and runny eggs.
Today I ran, my eggs untouched,
I ran toward the hideout, the border,
toward freedom, toward peace. I hope
on Mother's dirges as they accompany

my steps toward extinction. I watch
the world bleed from every angle,
every different pore, into chaos—

ASHES

I run as hungry flames chase us
from our homes. A hungry man
is an angry man. I run as fire
breezes through our paths.
The road now lined with oil and
years of labor fall into ashes.
I imagine the President's shady
promises about compensation.
Trucks ply broken roads.
Afar, gloomy smoke levitates
toward heaven. I spot some kids
laughing, playing *ten-ten*,
unaware of the wails nearby.
The fire roars in anger as if to
consume. I hate its wails
of loss. I close my eyes but
my nose, a Judas, breathes in
smoke. A dog barks
away, as if to express fury.
I know fire extinguishers
show up when it's too late. I recall
the Ikeja bomb blast and Dana Air
crash. I count tasbih of tragedies
until my fingers falter.
What legacy will this land leave?
What next will it take from us?
Nothing works here until there's
some damage. It is a bargain of
survival without a written treaty
that Nigeria won't still burn you.

LAND MINE

My brother surfs his iPhone as
the police halt our bus.

I signal to him but his mind wanders
to the net. I nudge his shoulder and

he shivers back to the bus.
I fear their eyes will pop to name him.

I'm used to this. My brother is not.
I've learned the road gimmicks by heart

like I know the new national anthem.
My eyes have seen things my tongue

locks in the bowels of my stomach
for what name do you give a country

that claws its youths by the neck?
Once, they dragged a boy by his ears

and handcuffed him for wearing locs.
His freedom dashed to the wind,

until there's enough to bail him out.
I want to teach my brother how

the cries of October 2020 dissipated
like sheer smoke into the blue sky.

When a youth goes missing here,
he has fallen headlong into thirst traps,

handcuffed to be led into a Black Maria
to waste away in Naija's Golgotha.

What is the future shape of our country
—our land mine that takes joy

in playing with the ashes of its youths?

DELIRIUM

Although we left,
I still remember how to walk on scattered bullets.
I fake sleep with a pillow covering my ear
to keep the deafening sounds of bombs away
the heart-wrenching screams of people dying outside the wall
their last words falling like leaves from a withering tree
—to become an enemy to those with whom you once shared
plates of pepper soup and drinks toasted to more life.
How do I blot out this unwanted phantasm in exchange for
flowery scents, seed pots, and Kunu? Yet my placenta lies there
and though we are miles away, across hills and seas
and time, they say heal, it is fifteen years now,
but I still jump out of sleep, hallucinating.

BURNT HOME GHAZAL

The ravens left feather prints in the clouds,
as tourists winged like migrant birds.
We hid and watched from mountaintops
as our men were hunted like pheasant birds.

Years before the crisis, the city flowed
with rivers of milk and honey.
Tranquil voices echoed daily in the streets
as our mothers sang like weaver birds.

Before the central mosque tasted the
wrath of an inferno by unknown gunmen.
The fire turned us hungry for blood,
we borrowed the feathers of mockingbirds.

Grandmother's ghost sat me at the table
and told me to live for today.
How do I dwell in the present when
the past lurks quietly like a whispering bird?

The world burned and burned,
by the flame in our unforgiven memories.
But won't the world keep burning unless
we learn from the hummingbirds?

We should take a thousand steps backward
to undo the past. It is not too late to wake
our dead, to find and heal our missing ones,
to sing and be merry again like happy birds.

My heart mourns this home of fire and ice
the pieces of peace smoking in the sky.
For what is so sweet about burning
and warring, about silencing wattlebirds?

THE SCULPTURE

Mother's album
drove me to the past:
running on the Rukuba hills,
sweet potatoes and fresh fruits,
click-clacks of pots and tasty steam,
shopping at the Terminus market in
between the stalls of noisy traders and
the sculpture of a woman with breasts
dangling sideways and a child strapped
to her back, faded always into space.
I hoped to touch her but we left in the
bloodbath of pines and tomatoes when
the crisis broke in the south-central
mosque. We left the shards of jolly
memories trapped forever in
the monumental pages of
mother's album.

EVERY TIME PLATEAU IS ON FIRE

I am as puzzled as the oyster
when I feel the sting of my identity
as both the victim and the gunman.

To identify with the guilty
and be a victim as well
is to lose my voice
in the cacophony of the mob's banter:
"Your people are killing others.
Your people are burning places.
You're a killer, too."

Yet those barbs do not make the
pointed fingers innocent, nor do they
douse the embers, nor wake
the orphan's parents
or feed or shroud the many displaced.

As a victim, I still fret every time I
remember that the last time I saw my uncle
was twelve years ago when he fled home
after shaving off his beard
and camouflaging in suits and ties
just to live to see the sun the next day.
I still wonder if he made it through.

IT'S SMOKY

My people are crying and I am waiting,
looking for a doorway to escape all of these.
The mouth of the wall has opened again
to swallow what is left of our hope.
See, there is a thing called hope.
It's like water cupped in a palm,
it doesn't stay put, that's how I see my country.

You do not want to call the country by
its father's name, long soiled in the mud by
the dirty hands of corruption.

Sometimes I forget it's not a nightmare
and I'm not living in my head.
Sometimes, I forget. It's crazy, this land.
It's smoky.
And I want to pretend that I'm asleep
but my eyelids—a Judas betrays me.
I'm forced to stare into the rubble again,
the rubble that is home.

Help, my lover is crying, he said,
I have written again of half-baked lands.

THE LEKKI TOLL GATE

Sometimes, I want to pray,
I want to say, *RIP*.
But my heart wouldn't tell souls
whose lives were unduly cut to rest in peace.
Today, I want to throw up a thousand words
but I am reminded by the radio in the cab
taking me to Lekki; in my country,
God is everywhere—down the streets,
in the schools, graveyards, and houses.
Fellowships take place in market squares, too.
There are more places of worship than schools.
In my country, God is everywhere
so there's no need for His space
in our hearts. He is the first
Word stamped on the tips of our tongues
but the last Word dangling on our hearts.
To my country's people, God is just another word.
A word for dying, a word for shock,
a word for awe, a word for fear,
a word for simply telling the truth, "Asweargod!"

Prayer in my country is a loud battle
with invisible enemies.
Sometimes, I fear how we curse ourselves,
fighting imaginary foes.
But I want to pray every time I pass the toll gate.
Until something like today's radio reminds me
that prayer is not the remedy
to my country's thousands of ailments.

Prayer isn't even the vaccine.
So I just whisper into thin air, "God forbid
this time bomb reaches my turn."
And then I sigh again and again
and say quietly, "Nigeria will not happen to me."

We found love in street protests

because we want to live and love and make flowery memories
all broken by stray bullets, by guns aimed at us.
we found love beckon to us in street protests

our country aimed at our lovers
our country drowned our dreams
in the Atlantic. shushed our voices with bullets.
we want to live to see the sunset and rainbow after the storm.
bask in the hearty scent of rain embracing the sands
walk to and fro our father's land calmly and not in needless fear.

our country was more silent than the cold bodies alive in Lekki
the hope the dreams trapped forever in the toll gate
the innocent flag drenched in betrayal of its blood
every morning we mourn our country in silence

peace and unity were our war song
shot dead on our lips.

PHANTOM

I hold this place with all of

its blue waters, dazzling sunlight,

tulips and bougainvillea—

I transcend to water,

curl around fleets of flowers.

Like a creek, unafraid,

I pour into others and the sea

mirrors the sky's vastness.

Beyond the shores, I see people

being people; not a single

White, Black, Yoruba, Muslim or Atheist.

Just people doing people things,

glowing in the absence of misfortunes

their dreams—colorful bubbles

curving into being.

I imagine my homeland as rivulets

that flow out of themselves

a home where wingless birds can

whirl about the sky;

where I can live in my skin without
the fear of its melanin coming off
an invitation to a cop's hungry bullet
whose eyes see my scarf as a detonator.

THE CITY'S BACK DOOR

Call me a prodigal running but
I am not. My eyes opened
and can now see the blurred lines.

It is perhaps true that you can't see
yourself until you step out of your skin.
But Nigeria does not need you

to step out before you see all its flaws.
They are right there, poking you in the eye.
I strived so hard to love here,

even with the desecration. Reminds
me of the innocent boy from the tutorials
before he wore a Yoruba man's crest.

Look, I do not know how to comfort
what I do not know how to love,
or what has decided to be unloved.

This country kills me daily
and my body is now dead from dying.
I try, I want to fall in love with her.

Again, my memory ricochets to
the boy from college, he too broke me.
Yesterday, I picked up the remnants

of my dreams and took a French leave
through the city's back door.
I am not a prodigal running.

SUNSET

The sun embraces us from her residence.
We have sinned against our souls and soils,
forgive our faults and let this hunger go down
with the setting sun.

We are rivers flowing into springs,
cliffs, and gulfs. We fall into ourselves—water.
No one resents water, may this thirst go down
with the setting sun.

We traded our dialect for slavery
and ravished our culture to corruption.
This land is ravaged, ruined, and wrecked.
The soils are tilled to impecunity,
the fruits are ripe and mildewed now.

We have seen our sins with our naked eyes,
they make us want to dig our soles into the carpet grass.
Embrace us and brace this race for us.